Animals from Head to Tail

HORSES FROM HEAD TO TAIL

By Emmett Martin

Gareth Stevens PUBLISHING

Please visit our website, www.garethstevens.com. For a free color catalog of all our high-quality books, call toll free 1-800-542-2595 or fax 1-877-542-2596.

Library of Congress Cataloging-in-Publication Data

Names: Martin, Emmett, author.
Title: Horses from head to tail / Emmett Martin.
Description: New York : Gareth Stevens Publishing, [2021] | Series: Animals from head to tail | Includes index.
Identifiers: LCCN 2019042314 | ISBN 9781538255360 (library binding) | ISBN 9781538255346 (paperback) | ISBN 9781538255353 (6 pack) | ISBN 9781538255377 (ebook)
Subjects: LCSH: Horses–Juvenile literature.
Classification: LCC SF302 .M2483 2021 | DDC 636.1–dc23
LC record available at https://lccn.loc.gov/2019042314

First Edition

Published in 2021 by
Gareth Stevens Publishing
111 East 14th Street, Suite 349
New York, NY 10003

Editor: Therese Shea
Designer: Laura Bowen

Photo credits: Cover, p. 1 Osetrik/Shutterstock.com; p. 5 Tim Platt/Digital Vision/Getty Images; p. 7 wakila/Getty Images; pp. 9, 24 (whiskers) LeliaSpb/Moment/Getty Images; p. 11, 24 (mane) Nora Carol Photography/Moment/Getty Images; p. 13 Kerrick/E+/Getty Images; p. 15 Gregory Johnston/Getty Images; p. 17 Hilary Helton/Photolibrary/Getty Images Plus/Getty Images; p. 19 Adam Davy - PA Images/Contributor/Getty Images; p. 21 Westend61/Getty Images; pp. 23, 24 (foal) Somogyvari/E+/Getty Images.

Printed in the United States of America

CPSIA compliance information: Batch #CS20GS: For further information contact Gareth Stevens, New York, New York at 1-800-542-2595.

Contents

Horses are large animals!

A horse's foot is one toe.
A hoof covers it.

A horse has whiskers. They help the horse feel things around it.

Horses grow long hair on their neck. It's called a mane.

They have a long tail.
It's silky.

Some horses pull heavy loads.

Some horses
carry people.
Police ride horses!

Galloping is a horse's fastest running.

Horses eat grass.
They eat hay and oats.

Horses have babies. The babies are called foals.

Words to Know

foal

mane

whiskers

Index